Raven

TO LOVE A WOMAN

Paul Marguglio

BALBOA.
PRESS
A DIVISION OF HAY HOUSE

Scripture quotations marked KJV are from the Holy Bible, King James Version (Authorized Version). First published in 1611. Quoted from the KJV Classic Reference Bible, Copyright ©1983 by The Zondervan Corporation.

Balboa Press books may be ordered through booksellers or by contacting:

Balboa Press
A Division of Hay House
1663 Liberty Drive
Bloomington, IN 47403
www.balboapress.com
1 (877) 407-4847

Print information available on the last page.

ISBN: 978-1-5043-3913-1 (sc)
ISBN: 978-1-5043-3915-5 (hc)
ISBN: 978-1-5043-3914-8 (e)

Library of Congress Control Number: 2015913368

Balboa Press rev. date: 08/28/2015

Dedicated to Love,
for to be in love is to experience every emotion.

Contents

Something About Sentiment

Acknowledgements

I want to thank Susan Barton and Michele Sloan for their support and encouragement.

I would also like to thank, Raven Ward who showed me how to care again. To share my thoughts and written verse. To remove my protective armor. To take a chance, that to feel isn't the same as feeling. She taught me that it was okay to let go the pain of the past, to live, to care, to trust. To trust your heart and most of all, to love a woman.

Introduction

As I held an old book of poems, pieces of the cover began to crumble in my hands.

Its tattered pages yellow from many years upon a shelf, longed to tell its tales of humor and sadness, peace and war, sentiment and reflection, love and love lost. Unlike my writings there is an end within these bindings and its inspiration will only last as long as the pages remain intact.

Though unfinished, my writings are a story of the encounters of two hearts cheated of eternal love. Yet there is a hope for a happy ending and it remains as a guiding light for words that may yet fill the still empty pages. These words, meaningless to some, may have particular value only to those who have shared similar life experiences. Even though all that I have written can be left to interpretation, it matters only that you alone understand what I have been trying to say. All that is obvious and all the hidden meanings trapped within rhyme and verse is worthless if it means nothing to you. These pages too, will one-day turn to dust and its words eventually forgotten, but the love that made it so will live eternally, eternally in the stars, eternally in the wind, eternally in the spirits that inherit the earth.

Something About Humor

Homer

Hector, a Trojan Prince was killed
by Achilles, which is probably why
they called him a heel!

Message For A Recorder

"Hello" "Hi it's me!"
It's important that I let you..
mumble, mumble, mumble, mumble,
mumble, mumble, mumble, on the
14th mumble, mumble, mumble,
mumble, mumble, mumble, mumble,
so if you should have any questions,
just give me a call at, mumble,
mumble, mumble, mumble, mumble,
mumble, mumble, I'll see you later.
CLICK

Unstressed Not

To this day I'm not a saint
I always use some self-restraint
but sometimes slip to much complaint
when I use the word ain't.

At some risk of sounding daint
I may not be or is it mayn't
to speak with such distraint
and keep from using ain't.

In some place with the name Geraint.
The town may be kind of quaint,
although its influence attaint,
a well known place, it ain't

And from this picture that I paint,
it's not so easy to being feint,
with these problems you can acquaint
but I could tell that you ain't.

The type that needs constraint,
to speak with just a little bepaint
and you probably sit when feeling faint,
so impressed, I ain't.

And while listening to the plaint,
I find myself besaint
to search a dictionary for depaint
Just to keep from using the word ain't

Imagine using weren't for ain't,
or trying to rhyme aren't with ain't.
Is not, are not am not ain't,
It's just easier using ain't......
Ain't it?

The Computer

The computer cannot do to humanity
what the clock has already done.

Workstation

This stupid computer is a real
piece of....knock, knock, tap, tap
on the screen, you're going in
the dumpster....bang, bang, tap, tap'
on the key, this hunk of junk is
not working.....rap, rap, tap, tap,
on the printer. Ah, it must be this
button here, knock, bang, rap, tap,
cause I know it isn't me!!

Halloween

On this night in chilled October
Could have been seen if I were sober.
The moonlight march of clanking bones
And eerie sounds of imprisoned moans.

Gargoyles overlook the shady lane
That leads to a dark ghostly domain
Of resting souls both young and old.
Beneath the earth, stiff and cold.

So wrong to think the dead are sleeping
Or really entombed for our safe keeping
They yearn to give their bones a chance.
To swing and sway at the graveyard dance.

One by one the gravestones moved
How or why could not be disproved
That departed souls could rise and stand
Let alone dance, I've seen first-hand.

The matted earth began to rise
As the dead appeared to my surprise
Creeping in their shredded apparel
Muttering tones of a Halloween Carol.

And skeletons danced beneath the moon
As the battered band played out of tune
To the clanking bones grinding and bumping
And ghastly images gliding and jumping

Dancing all night to the Boo-Ga-Loo
The monster mash and the two-step too
And little goblins played their pranks
While tired old ghost left their ranks.

When horrible screams filled the air
The crypt keeper shouted to end the affair
And patches of sod slowly upturned
The dead to their graves quickly returned

In perfect order their bones fell in place
As gravestones returned not showing a trace
With a sighing relief I finished my beer
The dead were all resting for another year
So how did I get here, I just can't remember
Must have missed that turn last September
Although I have tried, I cannot leave
Looks like I'm here to stay, hmm I do believe.

Tired myself, I felt like sitting
On my back, my bones were misfitting
The dirt and grass started covering my head
I can't help to think, this is it, I am.....

Oval Room

Bill smiled as he leaned back in his big leather
chair and put the cigar in his mouth.
Suddenly his face cringed and he spit the cigar to the floor.
As he wiped his mouth, he stated; that cigar taste like crap!
Monica giggled and said;
Turn it around!

The Haiku (Hokku)

Hamburgers

Hamburgers flat, round
sizzle within dancing oil
brown slowly, slowly.

Halloween

Jack-O-Lantern lights
A path to shadowed doorways
Of the Bates Hotel.

Howling winds, ghost sing
The devil follows your way.
Do not slow your step.

Listen to the night,
It is coming to you soon,
Fright beneath the moon.

Hot Dogs

Tube-steaks long and round
Do not bark, bite, or devour
But are devoured.

Rain

Standing in the rain
Without a cap or cover
Dampens clothes and thoughts.

What Sense

Clouded horizon
People think without a brain
The earth turns anyway.

Life

The pleasure of love
The scent of an open rose
The pain of death.

Follow Me

While contemplating way to make money,
a friend told me to take something that
belong to someone else.
After being punished, I became angry
with my friend for misleading me!

"e sempre meglio riflettere"
(second thoughts are always best)

Something About Love and War

Second Chance

If I had a chance to know you now
Would you look like a Jersey Cow?
Chewing your cud, sweeping the floor
Your kids tracking in mud, not closing the door
Or would you be tall and thin
Looking down on this life that I'm in.
Wearing furs 'round your neck
And rings on your fingers
Not giving a heck
With a scent that lingers.
Though sometimes I think
The grass may be greener
My thoughts quickly sink
When I remember you're meaner
Than the one who bewitched
The fields where I lay
It's too hard to switch,
So these fields will I stay.

Inverse Melody

To know what comfort is a friend
and take what could never blend
as heard in Hermit's songs
But not the daughter that belongs
to Mrs. Jones whose smile
can cure those ills for awhile,
with something that could never end.
To show what fortune is a friend.

My Love Will

When mountains of steel turn to rust
My love will shine like silver and gold
When seas have dried and turned to dust
My love will refine and never grow old
When winds have died and sun burns low
My love will sweep through barren space
To light your world in passions glow
And hold you close in warm embrace.

Did You Know

The temperature of the sun is 11,000 degrees Fahrenheit, but it cannot compare with warmth that comes from your heart.

And did you know that humming bird's wings beat about eighty times per second, which is so fast it looks like a blur but certainly not as fast as my heart when you are near?

Did you know that sugar is a class of sweet soluble crystalline carbohydrate, but it does not compare to the sweetness of your lips?

Did you know that silk is a fine soft shinny fiber, produced by silkworms and worn by royalty and that your hair is much finer, softer and is produced and worn only by you?

Did you know that your smile can chase away the rain and that your gentle touch can ease a hurt buried deep inside a soul?

Did you know that when you are near me, the summer's heat doesn't feel near as warm and the winter's chill doesn't feel near as cold because of you?

Did you know that on a clear night that all the stars in heaven twinkle like the lights of millions of Christmas trees, and when the moon rises smiling, it seems to be much larger and shine much brighter just because of your presents?

Did you know that being just you, is everything that could ever be, everything I could ever want? And when you are gone the emptiness in my heart is vaster than all the heavens and darker than the blackest night.

Did you know that I love you! I have loved you for as long as I remember. I cannot remember not loving you. I have known you before life, in another time, in another realm. I love you more now than I have ever before, yet I know now more than all else, you should know that I will always love you. I shall love you forever and ever more.

If Love

If love is the sin of a fool-
then virtue is the kiss of death.

Just A Dream

I have been to a world of dreams
where all is calm and trees are green
slightly moved by soft currents of air.
The sun shining in the teal blue sky
outlined by soft white clouds.
The air is so fresh and clean that it
gives you a feeling of intemperance,
stimulating every part of your body.
The rolling hills of gray, fall to the
open fields brilliant green, patched in
brown, sprinkled with flowers of pink
and yellow which go hand in hand to
meet the ocean's waves without sound.
The neutrality of nature.
Combined in all is the ultimate in peace
and tranquility.
Nothing seems to be very young or does
it seem to be very old.
It is not a place to hear a cry and not
a place to hear a clamor.
You can neither feel heat nor cold,
sadness or hate,
Just contentment
And you are there in this wonderful
world of dreams. In all your magnificent
splendor, you are there.
The texture of your hair is that of silk,
yielding to your every movement.
Your eyes, the color of love, expressing
kindness and affection, telling of
compassion and sincerity.
A glow reaches out from the inmost depths

of your heart, a heart as delicate as love
with a radiance warmer than the sun and
as constant as time.
Your tender smile, possessed of deep
sensibilities, reaches out to the very
essence of my soul.
Your enchanting lips enslave me to
your every whim.
Your appearance, like a spiritual being
of celestial purity, a goddess of all
existence, the world is at your feet.
Though just a dream, you are there.
For without you; there would be no
World, there would be no dream.
Because, you see.....
You are my world of dreams.

Remembering, is good and bad.

Star Lost

Where are you little star
What fate or fortune do you hold?
That I may see your light afar
In golden beams should it unfold?

Imperfection?

To My Special Angel:

You question why I believe you to be so perfect.

My opinions are based on what I have experienced, what I have seen and learned about life and about you.

I believe you are the most beautiful thing I have ever held in my arms. Your warmth and affection has been the root of my life's passion. You have the ability to enhance my every emotion and stimulate all of my senses. Not wanting to share you, I am envious of those who would steal you away. Your embrace is a sanctuary within the insanity and turmoil of daily life, providing both the peace and tranquility necessary for me to endure this existence. Combined with your touch, your voice can soothe the pain of a bruised knee or the throb of an aching heart. Your kindness exceeds all that I have ever known, you have the patience of a saint and your generosity comes truly from your heart. Your beliefs in truth and honesty are hindered only by your concerns for the feelings of others. Your caring goes beyond self-sacrifice and your sincerity is a glowing beacon from your soul. Others are drawn to you because of this eminence of awareness and you are destined to inspire compassion in every heart you touch. You are hurt by the souls that do not receive you, but you should not let this discourage your spirit because even God cannot reach all.

Should it be a consideration, your only flaw is being human.

Is it no wonder that I love you so?

Let Me

Let me love you for a little while
So that I may joke to make you smile
Say clever things to let you see
How truly devoted my love can be.

I'll shield you from unwanted pain
Cover you from the falling rain
Keep you warm when it gets cold
And be your love until we are old.

I'll love you even when we are apart
Love you with every beat of my heart
As long as the ocean meets the shore
I'll love you forever and ever more.

But if your love I cannot win
The distant star shall burn within
A crystal tear, in the sky above
Becoming the light of everlasting love.

Softest Hour

Gathered to the softest hour
Without a wind or wave
All the heart could ever devour
An endless love to enslave.

With Love

To walk with love on a day in spring
The beauty of love is a wondrous thing
Feel the comforting warmth the sun does bring.

To walk with love is to hear the birds sing
To walk with love is to smell the flowers in the air

And see that which is so fine and so fair
A taste of life that we could share
To walk with love is beyond compare

To walk with love is nature's virtue
The magnificent are far and few
But most of all it is very true
To walk with love is to walk with you.

Glass Hour

Very slowly passes the hour
Til again into your eyes I'll gaze
Times weight on love cannot deflower
To time we are but lowly slaves.

Change

I'll never forget the day
Into my life you came
I think that I could surely say
My life will never be the same.

Be My Valentine

I have never seen you in the morning
light or under a moonlight sky.
I can only imagine a beauty as bright
or the starry twinkle in your eye.
I've never sat and talked with you
to explain to you how I feel.
I can only hope for a word or two
to make this all seem real.
I've never walked with you hand in hand
or held you tightly in my arms.
I can only imagine your warm embrace
expressing all of your charms.
I've never seen you sad with grief
or your eyes filled with tears.
I can only hope that you will always
be happy throughout your years.
I've never seen you happy with joy
a moment we may have shared.
I can only say your happiness I'll enjoy
and believe you may have cared.
I may never know the taste of your lips
or the secrets of your heart.
I can only wish a mighty wish
that with a kiss, true love will start.
I may never know what your love may be
or ever see your brilliance shine.
I can only dream a wonderful dream
and hope someday you will be mine.

Shining Star

Oh shining star with beauty bright
Your love through darkness beams
From heavens way in warm delight
To keep you always in my dreams.

Whisper by My Window

I saw you pass my window
And I wondered what you are.
Are you just a passing light
Or the reflection of a star?
Are you soft and gentle
Like a fragile flake of snow
Whose sparkling crystals glisten
And yet will never know
What warmth may be in a heart
As glowing cauldrons burn,
Lightly floating on winter winds
To melt away and never return?
Are you bright and lucent
Like a shimmering moonbeam
Peaking through fluffy clouds
Dancing wildly on a stream,
To stray with nightly shadows
Prancing until the dawn,
Embracing another moonbeam
With the morning sun be gone?
Are you sweet and subtle
Like the petals of a rose,
Whose luring fragrance calms
A restless heart to repose,
Only to be pierced by thorns
An already bleeding soul
Pour its liquid for your color
Flower of red I do extol.
Are you pure and lovely
Like an angel high above
Whose tender truth and kindness
Is an assurance of lasting love,

Though mingled in saintly praise
With less wanted love returned
Your purpose above a common need
But to keep a soul unburned?
Are you just a vision
An apparition in the night,
Appearing in phantom beauty
Only to vanish from my sight?
Do I just see your image?
Please, to me yourself reveal
Are you the lady of my heart
Are you really real?

Sleight of Heart

While thinking about stealing a kiss
And taking your heart
You took mine and
I didn't know it.

Juliet

My Dearest Juliet;

Your way has found my heart and lifted its rusty beat from the waste at the highways edge.

You have polished its shell so that it could shine among the stars, to where even the moon has become envious of its luster.

My effulgence is such, that I cannot be overshadowed by the sun.

You have given me the brightness to sparkle even on still waters.

I have twinkled through the wagons spokes and sparkled in the spider's web.

I have rested my beam upon the mountains peaks and fallen upon the silence of slumbering faces.

I have warmed weary bones and have made little creatures sit up at night.

And nesting birds have I deceived to be the morning light.

I have raced with joy through the open air, spreading my colors in the midst of a spring shower.

I have laughed aloud without a care and lifted a crown to the ivy tower.

I have swept through scented amber fields to touch the petals of a rose.

Even darkened clouds, I would not yield, to see the starlight twinkle upon your nose.

I have danced about the woodland trees, traveled to the oceans depths.

I have lingered in the somber sky and flickered when you have wept.

I have seen the rainbow of your smile, glisten in droplets of dew.

Yet in my heart, I have known all the while, my shine is just a reflection from the brilliance of you.

I Love You

Valentine

On this special day there are so many ways to say, I LOVE YOU. I can use a card that may have a picture of a red heart, or cupid drawing his bow. Inside the card may be words describing my eternal love and my undying devotion and I can also give you flowers. Sentimental though it may seem, it is hardly enough that I should only give you a card and flowers on St Valentine's Day to express how and why I am so deeply in love with you.

I know that it isn't necessary to prove how I feel about you, yet I do feel the need to share what I think and I want to remind you of what you mean to me.

You are my truest friend, caring for me when I am happy or sad, understanding when I am angry or afraid and loving me in spite of my imperfections. You stand by me when my world turns upside down, you listen to me when I need to talk and you fill my arms when I need someone to hold. When I question the whys and where's of life and doubt my own existence I need only to look into your eyes and all my questions disappear. Being with you is all I ever think of and having your love is my greatest desire. When I see you I see a radiant beauty of spiritual essence glowing about your form. Your brilliance guides my way and inspires my soul to a higher awareness. I am becoming a better person by just being near you. When your hand touches my hand I feel a pleasurable electric sensation of caring and affection. This touch makes still my restless emotions, giving me peace and serenity. When I hold you in my arms I feel the warmth of your heart and the goodness of your soul uniting our physical entities as our spirits become complete. When we kiss, the world around us fades away and only that which is true reality remains. I believe as we grow together and the combination of our elements becomes whole, our love will overcome the boundaries of life and we will move closer to the ultimate perfection.

Destiny has brought us together and our faith is the bond that holds us as one. I want to be everything you have ever wanted, I want to be everything you will ever need. You are my dream come true, my angel and I love you will all of my heart.

Will you be my Valentine?

Love Always And Forever

Your Beauty

On rolling waves of flowered fields
The earth your beauty fills
Within your heart your goodness yields
A sea of liquid daffodils.

To The Devils Dismay

There is a love transcending time
And although the clock continues
In its pace, eventually stealing youth
And deepen the lines upon our faces,
It cannot steal the root of this passion
For true love will only deepen, even
When autumn the leaves become silent.
The sun will slip below the horizon,
Never to thaw the shackles that bind
Us to these unpleasant memories.
And though the distant star shines
Upon the sweet angel and the poet,
It is left to the burning flame within
Our hearts to fade to dust the ghost,
That villainous spirit and melt away
These bonds which will set us free.

When Love Dies

A misplaced passion from a love renewed
must dry those tears and burn the past from a
mind that struggles still with all those surly spirits.
For the madness locked within a broken heart
has paid a thousand fold for every empty virtue
and though the white dove has shed a tear for this
cremation, the ashes cast upon the sea so long ago
that whatever was burned and why has become
meaningless. Yet the pain still lingers and the
white dove, also hurt, has long since flown away.
The remaining dust will swirl in the currents
of the changing airs to settle on earth and sea.
Then, what seems like a voice echoing from the
castle walls, will fade to sounds resembling an
infants cry. And life for some will go on, only
to exist in emptiness and others will just die.

Misplaced

As we face yet another test, it is again
the past that challenges these bonds.
Though fragile, it's the story of our past
that serves alone as a moral adhesive.
So how do we separate the past from
the present and the good from the bad?
And once started, this surgical separation,
should all that is divided become equal?
So does the devil and his staff delight
to steal us from heavens shining light
and turn us to these villainies of nature,
Compounding what is lost in endless pain.
Premature repairs to a skeletons closet unfold
today and yesterday in misplaced passion.
Then shall the lover perish, when this love
is gone. Only then realizing the loss.

To Love You Not

To love you not, I don't know how
Or to love you less than I do right now
To care for you not, I could not pretend
Or even think of you just as a friend.

In loving you less could be what effect
To the earth and sky, I could not reject
A heart so pure, I would rather instead
Surrender my life and think of me dead.

Play It Again

As time goes by this ancient tune
Of silver screen, shredded and strewn
Plunks tinny notes from ivory keys
To tears that flow with sorrowful ease.

Brings back once more that precious kiss
From lips so sweet and soft that this
Old fire inside burns so intense
Fear and pain fades to indifference.

A kiss is still a kiss to remember
This love is still a burning ember
In moonlight and haze unto another day
A story without glory ends in disarray.

No matter what the future holds
Or memories, the past unfolds
A quest for love, to do or die
Amounts to dust as time goes by.

Mademoiselle

It was when in love with you I fell,
The day you came into my shell,
And cast on me your love spell.
A love that caused my heart to swell,
A day I noticed the flowers sweet smell.
In my mind and my heart you did excel,
The joys of life that you can't buy or sell.
Blinded by love we could not foretell
That never together we should dwell.
When last we meet was to be farewell.
And love's last love we should expel
The pains of love to learn so well,
Have put my soul in a flaming hell.
And taken my heart to tear and quell.
My soul echoes like a broken bell,
While my heart pounds with a mournful knell.
My mind encased in an impassive cell,
Deprived the need to cry or yell.
But, love is more than words could tell,
I learned when in love with you I fell.

Just You and Me

I'm as happy as can be
When we're together
Just you and me.

The sun never shines as bright
Or is the sky as blue
And my heart never feels as light
As it does when I'm with you.

Yes....I'm as happy as can be
When we're together,
Together forever,
Just you and me.

First Kiss

That first kiss, so sweet and true
A kiss so deep and felt all through
Vanished all fear, awakened my heart
I wished that never our lips to part.

As voices of angels grew in my head
A silvery bloom and fear I was dead
So perfect and warm it illumed my soul
No human can feel and remain in control.

My pulse rapid as bells started ringing
And softly angels in heaven began singing
Shutter and trembling within your embrace
My heart beating wildly, at such a rapid pace.

My soul shouted as it soared high above
My mind told my heart, this must be love
Though partly afraid and somewhat dismayed
Would this kiss last or eventually fade?

The tear on your check, although it was mine
Impressed such with love, I cannot define
That first kiss so tender, will always remain
In my heart and my mind until we kiss again.

Again First Kiss, (ten years after)

So many years have come and gone
At times it was hard to carry on
Without your warmth and tender kiss
Your gentile touch I will forever miss.

Time and distance has kept us apart
But you will always have a piece of my heart
And ever I wished your love to reclaim
When our lips meet will that kiss be the same?

Or with this kiss, would this dream end
Or heavenly spaces would this kiss send.
Our hearts and minds to be joined as one
Forever in love and to be never alone.

The time grows near, until we kiss again
But this growing fear can drive you insane
Though deep in my heart, I always knew
That precious my love, could only be you.

Each Time You Leave

When I look into your eyes
I can feel my heart soar
Into heavenly skies
As it did once before
And this feeling so grand
Is like walking on air
Would holding your hand
be so unfair?

When I hear your sweet voice
I tingle inside
For you as my choice
How long have I tried
Oh this wish in growing
To leave all behind
Within a love glowing
Could it be so blind?

When I hold you tight
I feel so at ease
Like wind in the night
Through the swaying trees.
For when you are near
You become the light
Dispelling the fear
Of not being right
And warm is your touch
For the moment secure
In loving you such
Could be so unsure.

I cannot atone
To the changing day
I just feel alone
When I see you walking away.

IF

If I could catch a rainbow
I would give it to you
To cool a lost desire.

If I could touch your heart
I would give you my soul
To revive a dying fire.

If I could reach the sky
I would wrap you in a soft
And silky gentleness.

If I could do all of these things
I would wish for you
Faith, Love and Happiness.

A Christmas Wish

I have made a wish beneath a bright star in heaven.

I wished for a snowflake to carry my dream, giving to you as a gift, the whole of my being. I want to give you my heart and my forever love and dedicate the rest of my life to your happiness. My greatest desire is for your true love. I want to experience your faithful heart, to feel your gentle touch and your warm embrace, to kiss your sweet lips and listen to the kindness and sincerity of your voice. I want to know that our love is real, that we are forever one and forever in love. I want to let you know how very important you are to me. I want to help you with daily chores and do simple things like zip up your dress or hold a mirror when you need an extra hand, maybe brush your hair when your arms get tired, or just rub your feet when you have had a long day. I want to be by your side and hold your hand so that you know I am there for you. I like to watch you sleep and be near you when you open your eyes. I want to kiss the tears from your cheeks when you are sad and enjoy your laughter when you are happy. Our spirits have been linked in such a way that the link between us will forever keep us together. These hopes are part of a dream, riding on a crystal snowflake and the snowflake brings a wish and the wish is that on Christmas morning we may sit under the same tree and open a present together and know that the dearest gift we share is our love.

Imagine

Imagine there were no stars above
Or sun or moon up in the sky
Living in a world without love
Or birds that couldn't fly.

No desert sand or fertile land
Where trees and flowers could grow
No city streets where buildings stand
Or winter valleys covered with snow.

Imagine all the little things
No creature, big or small
No loving hearts where beauty sings
Not a living soul at all.

Not a mountain peak or ocean blue
To pound upon the shore
That's what life would be without you
Much more than I could endure.

Not Alone

You're not alone
In a world unkind
With flesh overthrown
And control of mind
Hold to your spirit
Meant to be free
It cannot submit to
An obsessive trustee
As passion in place
Of love just a part
You cannot retrace
Or fix a broken heart.

Waiting

I asked the sun today if you would come to me,
but it just turned away and I could only see,
the golden sphere disappearing in the sky,
behind passing clouds as all above began to cry.

The day is shadowed in a gothic gray and the entire world seems hushed by a gentle rain falling ever so lightly through the trees. Looking through a window, everything appears to be lingering in a peaceful remoteness as the scattered streams upon the window distort a vision of yesterday.

With early signs of fall, the warm summer days are rapidly coming to an end. Sad summers end, so sad will it pass in memories of warm pleasant smiles and the soft touch of a delicate hand. Soon the trees will change in a colorful portrait of nature's kindness and this summer will become a bittersweet memory. Fall will sojourn until the first cold wind and the winter will grasp this world with deliberate unfriendliness. A season of untouchable beauty, its lack of warmth and affection will seem even colder because you are not here.

My window has changed and through it comes a chill of the days ahead.

I asked the stars tonight if you would come to me
but standing in the twinkling light, I could only see
another sphere beginning to fill the sky as
the moon rose smiling and I began to cry.

Waiting Still

I asked the sun today if you would be calling me,
but it just turned away and I could only see,
this wish in dying hope, dry in the callus sun
and clouds that form when the day is done.

Once in a while there is a compulsion to pursue the distant star
only to be lost in the reminiscent swirl of the silent sky.
A poetic creation of the mind that becomes nothing more
than a fanciful assumption and what is lost or gained is seen
in a melancholy view of dusty fields or falling rain.
The sky painted in uneven textures, blends with billowing clouds
and golden beams from contrasting horizons, to balance the heavens
between ominous apprehension and extreme elation.
Somewhere in the realm of this visionary speculation is a portal
to acceptance and a place of perfection next to an angel.
This day began in a dramatic portrait of nature's beauty and it
will end in the pitiless gloom of another night.
The night, dark and lonely, will seem oh so empty because
you are not here. I miss you so, I miss you.

I asked the stars tonight if you would be calling me
but standing in the twinkling light, I could only see
the stars being melted by the dawn to a ringing phone
and a call with your voice, I'm no longer alone.

This Voice

What is this voice from afar
Through the heavens past the star
To sing and whisper in musical chimes
Then turn and listen to poetic rhymes?

It is a melodic mystery I part
Keeping the secrets of your heart
Composed of thought and feeling
A symphony of words so unrevealing

That this voice from so far away
Can brighten such an empty day
With funny gestures across the miles
Through callus air bringing smiles.

Even though you're hardly near
It's the sweetness in your voice I hear
Gentle tones from a mountain view
In warm delight are thoughts of you.

Tear On My Window

The morning sun cloaked in gray
Casting shadows upon the day
No glory blooms in twilight air
Or golden beams upon your hair

And from the tree, no robins song
So empty shall the day seem long
Without you touch what can remain
Is seen in gentle falling rain

Upon the window in scattered streams
Through the trees in clouded streams
To slow the pace of life so rushed
Peaceful, as the world is hushed

To memories of a summer past
In hope, forever will they last
As nature paints a summer's tree
In autumns color, to its kindness see

That this world will the winter grasp
Through my window my heart clasp
Without your warmth there comes a chill
To make the cold yet colder still.

For your love

Tonight, when you are falling asleep
should you hear a whisper, it will be
me making a wish.

Suborn

When I listen to the kindness
of your words, do I sit in blindness?
But yet I heard, another voice
from your lips, another choice
for your kiss, as your fingers
touched my lips, never lingers
from your kiss, so do we play
our part, that we may stay
apart from someone we have not met
though this feeling is alive and yet
only few words are spoken.
So sad a heart may be broken.

Never Say Good-bye

In my days I've seen
A person who was quite as keen
Oh so pleasant to behold and know
That always will your virtue show
A quality so immensely fine
The smile in your heart will forever shine.

And in this moment of grim parting
Sensing the feeling of loneliness starting
I try to find the words to say
Expressing the happiness you put in each day.
But more difficult does come each verse
And an emptiness does my heart immerse.

Behind the bonds of closing doors
A dream of dreams is forever yours.
For it's not wrong to redeem
A part of love that is a dream
And yet to be departed friends
All that begins, also ends.

From the night from which is drawn
The morning light of the golden dawn
And past days from what has been taken
Shall flourish once more when we awaken.

Let not a shedding tear be fallen
For not ever shall we cry
And not a parting kiss be given
For we never say good-bye.

Now at this moment of sweet sorrow
And each passing hour through
Spreading happiness till the marrow
Preserving in my heart the loveliness of you.

Significant

A rain drop is such a small part of the ocean
A tear drop is such a large part of the soul.

Love Again

Take me back I so that I might see
A love, my love so true to me
A smile so kind and eyes that cared
A love true love, a love we shared.

Take me back so that I might know
How winter winds bring flakes of snow.
How rainbows form after a summer rain
How it would be to kiss your lips once again.

Take me back so that I might feel
The things in life that are really, real
Of all the past to close the door
To hold you in my arms once more.

Take me back so that I might find
A love, true love that I left behind.
To place my heart within your view
And spend the rest of my life loving you.

If I Kissed Your Cheek

You say that your hair messy
But it looks okay to me
It was only stirred a light
Breeze, coming from the sea.

You think your voice is raspy
But I didn't hear anything wrong
Could be something like a little cold
Though what I hear is a song.

I see that your eyes are red
You've been crying for awhile
If I could tell you a funny story
Do you think it would make you smile?

You say your heart is broken
And you are feeling sort of meek
I think you would feel much better
If I held you close and kissed your cheek.

A Thought

In the solace of my chamber thinking
My mind to thought slowly sinking
I search and search for a rhyming way
A thought for you that I could say.

There's not much to hello's goodbyes
And surely not to how's and why's
Of all the things we say and do
Requited thanks are reserved and few.

Plastic smiles on plastic faces
The shallow greeting of hand embraces
For people are not what they seem
And I cannot be the one to deem
The difference between what's good and bad
Or tell what makes us happy or sad
Noticing the trivial do's and don'ts
Imposing reluctant, I will's and won'ts.

There are those who may recall
And also those who won't at all
So, I'm no different from the rest
I can't even say that I tried my best.

Though my eyes may get a little red
I won't say much about what's done or said
To think about all the things we have seen
Or how it was or what might have been.

Yet to know what it may come to be
Not knowing whether we're lost or free
And grasping what has come or past
Seeking that pleasure that comes at last.

Within these bonds I fail to find
Something to say from my mind
It's hardly a wish I can implore
Just a thought from my heart and nothing more.

Parting Wish

Should your hands hold only the sweetest of roses
And your heart know only the truest love.
Should your eyes see only the beauty of life
And your soul know only heaven above.

Alone

I sit alone and wonder why
Should strings of amity we untie
Standing, staring into the sky
Remembering the sad tear in your eye
All I could do is give a sigh
Remembering sadly our last goodbye.

A Birthday Wish

Even though I am not there with you on your special day, I want you to know; know in your heart, that my thoughts and my spirit are with you. I wish that I could be there to watch you blow out the candles on your birthday cake, so I may see the joy on your face and share in the happiness of your wonderful day. I know when the candles go out and the room darkens, you will be able to sense my presence and feel my love and know that my birthday wish is reaching out to touch your soul. Though my spirit is sad, it can wait forever. It is my physical self that must learn to endure.

I will visit my memories often, during this time without you and rest in comfort reliving the most pleasant thoughts that I could remember of the time I spent with you. I may wish to be with you but my wish for you is a hope that all of your wishes and dreams come true. Have the best birthday ever.

No Matter

No matter how tight you may close your eyes
A tear will always find your cheek.

Empty Place

The distance wounds with tears
the heart whose love in phantom
dream so wings to earthly ends.
in a journey through fog and mist
beyond the sea to shores already
all so far. The stars above me
twinkle at your sun as specters stand
beside my bed to haunt a sinking
vision of an image in the sun.
these dreams of mine twist and
turn through hidden thorns, while
climbing a frozen peak above a
distant shore, only to find an empty
place, only to learn that you have gone.

You Passed Me By

You passed me by and I just watched you walk away
I thought of you for a while, with hopes of seeing you another day
You passed me by and I watched you fade from sight
I turned away only to think of you all through the empty night
You passed me by and graciously waved your hand in my direction
I turned away only closed my eyes to such beautiful temptation
You passed me by with a charming smile causing some despair
I turned away only because watching you go was so hard to bear
Then not passing me by you touched my soul for a time
Only to leave and take my heart to a mountain so hard to climb.

Love Is A Star

Love is part of life and life a part of time.

Time is every moment that ever was or will be
And life is bound within the fortress of time.

Love is a star and a star, a burning heart, captured
In the reminiscent swirl of the silent past.
Its light passes through a threshold of a distant
Dream, pursuing something which has flown away.
With its sparkling brilliance entangled within the
Binding of aspired visions, it resides in an
Elusive beam upon an imparted shore.
Becoming the center of lost emotions, it is
Reduced to simplicity in a fallen tear
Only to be remembered in a weighted sigh.

In a part of time we exist in life, and in life we
Will be loved and again we will love.

Parting Soul

Dear friend, devoted friend
whose greatness cannot save
this soul so doom, in quiet gloom
to keep it from its grave.

And friend, kind friend
your memory will I keep
within my heart, as we part
though bound to ever lasting sleep.

Good friend, gracious friend
mourn not the passing of this soul
in quelling earth, begins new birth
your heart it must console.

Caring friend, eternal friend
as the time to leave grows near
I feel God's hand, by his command
take away all of this fear.

Oh my friend, my precious friend
though this life is almost through
it was you path to clearing wrath
that held my way so true.

And now my friend, my loving friend
these lips may never reveal
a love in pain, that must remain,
how could this soul conceal
from you my friend, my beautiful friend
this truth in hope and fear
to survive alone, this love unknown

should die in a single tear
with love my friend, my worthy friend
to hide this from your view.
It was your faith that gave me faith
to love and live for you.

Again Passion

To think this verse has ended
shall together chime, in the hideous
ticking rhythm, forsaking the
regimented order of the clock.
A sematic semblance from the
past and from northern winds,
a stormy surge of winters
blistering chill, is warmed
by lost passion, reflecting
rippled images, not within a
flame but frozen in the mirrors
forgotten space, thought withering
in lighted memories, dimming so
very slowly in the fabric of time.

Reopened Book

Why, why has this spirit no pity
to unfold these girded pages,
tattered by time as dried leaves
crumbling from a touch unwanted,
imparting those lives in braided paths,
and knowing the saucy call was faint,
shall it echo in hollowed verse?
Again that angel dwells, nearly
within reach of trembling feelings,
nearly within sight of tired eyes,
only to be hopelessly resurrected
as undulating forms upon a wave,
only to quietly die again, in forgotten
ashes strewn upon a pitiless sea.

Again This Love

Oh this loathsome growth
invades the sweetest rose
with the chilling breath of chilling
beauty to deceive in separate
name, another love, so divided
in emotional torment and in pain.
Curse the shore with ruthless waves
to wash away the wasted years,
of sorrow, the wasted tears in vain
and curse the shadowy clouds that
cloak such wounds from redeeming
amber beams and curse the deadly
venom of those callous lips
bewitched of selfish love.

Fallible

These faults of men enslave
in grieving hell, a civil
war within the soul, expecting
prayer to excuse a sin,
expecting wounds to heal.
And how such deeds in
love and hate bring tears
from heavens way, to stain
the skies beyond the clouds
with swirls of dust from
bones so ruddied by the blood
of their own, only to be
discarded as less wanted waste
upon the threshold of a lost star.

Succumb

Damn this mortal life so distilled by
night and day so narrowly numbered in
fading delicate substance, despite the
desperate cries of lost hearts in ambit ambling.
What strength gains this nightly grief in
taking this image of sagging flesh in
painted portraits upon the hollowed walls,
mended graciously by the artist hand,
to unmask the offending thief of time
so that we may see its face, for virtue
does your visage conceal a tyrant that
we may bare its lines, eventually
surrendering, to lie in sweetened earth and
beckon weary bones to meadows green.

Deliverance

Another night steals the east
another sleepless night so
bewailed by stars in shining
from a faraway distant shore
so placid from the elusive dream.
Take this anger in a deepest plea
upon the wings of angels, to
unweight a broken heart in gentle
closure and let this mind in wistful
journey peacefully rest, rest in ease
of night to soothe this tired woe,
hopefully, to awake smiling and
kiss the golden face of morning.

The Conflict

To be one within oneself
but not alone upon a shelf
extending to a greater plain
with some pointless speech to regain,
can free from this hellish woe
so clean a sharpened pen may show
that life alone surfeit despair
an empty heart cannot compare
the hunger of the burning beast
upon these dying heats feast.
With penury passion consuming fire
Yet drowned within a lost desire
bid farewell from lips so parted
in ashes of the broken hearted
So bewitched does this remain
untainted to a kiss in vain.

The Struggle

Unstirring time with mercy flow,
a past in phosphorescent glow,
serves only to slow this pace
for nothing is the mirror's space.
From vacant vigilance unthrowned,
by grappling ghost disowned,
quietly, to besmirch this moral good
credulous, that your virtue could,
oppose a vow and still believe
times cruel indenture to deceive,
enslaving the valiant love devotion,
infinitely spiral, descending emotion.
Though faint, this light in burning
not forget, just end a yearning,
in a binding calm of sorrow,
must let go before tomorrow.

Breaking Free

Oh where does this spirit dwell
perplexing airs between heaven and hell,
in the numbing coarseness of the cold,
or eternal deaths unfriendly hold?
Consecrated tribute to faithless bound,
lie peacefully wrapped in holy ground,
hover seven angels overhead,
with voiceless blessings for the dead,
unearthing souls and stones unturned,
for there is nothing left to burn.
Out last ember, out forever then,
free this heart to love again.
And utter not an empty prayer,
for only stars and saints can bear,
the loss and sorrow in such grief,
divinely healed in new belief.

RED BANK

Lonely soldier by the river bed
guarded by cannons rusty and old
monument of stone for those who bleed
and where you died your story is told.

Lonely soldier by the river bed.
A park they've made your battle ground.
River banks where charges led,
Now people just come to walk around.
They care not about those who are dead,
They forget the cries of the battle sound,
They care not about the blood you shed,
They see not what I have found.

More than rusty cannon,
green grass or tree.
More than rolling hill or
river flowing out to sea.
A stone engraved a battle fought
that left our banks in red.
Here lies a lonely soldier,
lonely soldier by the river bed.

Christmas Wish 2001

Christmas, celebrated around the world in many different traditions and customs, is a holiday of festivity and rejoicing. Among all the meanings of Christmas there is a message bearing the key to life and the destiny of mankind.

A tree decorated with lights and ornaments may be the rally point for the exchanging of gifts and fellowship. The story of Christmas will be told, and some will rejoice to a new king and a chapter in God's plan and others will fail to grasp it meaning. There will be shopping and parties, sending of cards, food and drink, singing of carols, an old guy in a red suit, carrying a sack, there will be cookies on a stool with a glass of milk, a toy for a child, a scarf for a mom, a tie for a dad, and a petition to the world for peace and goodwill. A prayer can be heard for the salvation of mankind in the beat of a drum and a sounding trumpet. There is hope for humanity and the key is giving.

Wishes begin beneath a bright star in heaven, and I wish for you a happy holiday season.

Merry Christmas.

The War After

And nothing can you call this death
for its meaning is our own to choose
what God and country we will serve.
For our cause is just and divine
though war is lost in peace and
and peace is war, while the hardship
feeds the burning hunger bitter bread.
Even now those rolling drums
sound glories call to gilded gloom
and dismal sorrow, stands firm
in naked honor, as before,
making dust of a soldiers will
to end upon the wall, only to etch
in brittle ebony, another name.

China Beach, China Doll

Seen waiting for the sun
under a starry sky
do clowns with porcelain
tears upon red cheeks glazed
cold and eyes unblinking
look to a dream unknown.
In hardened tenure,
do these watchmen stare over
a sea, so deep and dark
light has no color and creatures no
substance yet these hollow figures
of themselves shall expire like sand
in waves upon pebbled shores to change
their place as do the night and day.

Battle Stress

Locus ceruleus systems trigger
central to the brain an active
warning, stimulating control
of centers major hormone norepine-
phrine, which turns the key to
bloodstream flow adrenocortico-
trophic release to dilated eyes
and erected shafts of hair as
muscles contract and widen for
the need of blood, the heart beats
faster as pressure begins to rise
with tides of sugar no longer digest
in liquid red, clotting to air the skin
vessels contract and quickly pale
reacting to the stress of battle.

The Mask

The M17A1, is a field protective mask.
consisting of the following M17 series
components; face-blank, M15 carrier
assembly, M1 waterproof bag, eye lens
outserts, M1 canteen cap. Also in the
enclosed are optical inserts, M6A2
hood and M4 winterizing kit. The M17A1
has a matched pair of filter elements
that will provide protection against
all known toxic agents, except ammonia
vapors, carbon dioxide, and heavy
concentrations of aerosolized particles
such as smoke mixtures. Change the filters
should they impose severe impedance to
breathing. The mask does not produce air.

Inside The Mask

Go away, go away oh aqueous ghost
how bitter is your breath, outside
the mask that filters clean in magic
form, right before these eyes and
nose, confined within face blank skin
and outserted lenses arranged in
weird dispose, protecting from this
ominous thing, hovering below pierced
heavens, shall I construe the meaning
of a clouding menace in the fashion
of a facial cover, in fixed expression,
grotesque in cold reflection, upon a
raw fear of rationed air, in a struggle
to maintain self-control and sanity.

Warfare, CBR

Grab your mask, you cannot hide
when heralds from the heavens flash
delivering in thundering warnings
serum fumes in ghostly clouds
making men fear and tremble
with concaved palms over your face
the suffocating threat grows real.
Put on the mask and close your eyes
to open fields of sunbeams warm
inhaling the filtered contamination
of gliding debacle erupting overhead
and breath, slowly breath clean breath
the metallic wind of certain end
drawn through a garrote, but clean.

Unwanted

The pretty rights that honor holds
binds to holy ground a dream
where melancholy fades with
no affection for human existence
for the madman goes unwatched
demanding tribute from those
he has confined, while spreading
fear in mothers' hearts, they cry.
Their young may die in a land
so far away, the sun shines
before the dawn and the earth
turns toward the sea in pitchy
death. A pitiful ambition
spawned from neglected love.

Haunting Cry

Still, so still this idle wind
hangs soft a mist in exiled
light from distant fired burn
above a swarthy earth so charred.
And metal eagles soar through
menacing skies as blazing chariots
rolling through tilt-yards armored
against a forging timbale.
Those clanging chains and headless
lions tantivy din from wordless
tongues, chill crystal blood in veins
from marrowless bones and eyes
of stone, stare from decaying
stratum, cold and still, so still.

Not Knowing

What is this death that overcomes
the sight of eyes and sounding
tones to ears that listen with
intent, ending sweet scents to
to flaring nostrils, straining to
recall a home cooked meal
or a lover left far behind.
What is this death that takes away
a warm smile to cool the skin
so the sunshine cannot warm it
and the body does not rise
for another act, but plays
a dawdie part in muting felicity
so cold, so pale, so still.

Way War

What pleasure can bring these deeds
within the gates of other hearts
to invade the sacred palace
of the soul with tormenting
pain and sorrow. Obscurely
melting, those precious words
into preordanance of freedom
a decree that uses the blood
of men to hold a place in hell
for the tyrants with power.
And even those who speak of
peace, then hide from harm shall
one day die in the debt of those
who marched with weapons and a cry
Liberty, Peace and Freedom!

Importance

Does it matter?
that the sun may never shine
upon those faces and souls
who march to drums in desert sands
weaving a chain of sorry.
Trained so, these valiant soldiers
yare to battle gallantly
to fight this empty ass whose
crest deceives the promise of
peace in obscure sentences.
And with a single drop of blood
that blends with worthless sand
ignites a change in value exceeding
any fortunes makes it so.

Christmas Wish 2003

There are many in Afghanistan unfamiliar with the celebration of Christmas and there are many in Afghanistan, Iraq and many other parts of the world, who will know all to well what it is like to be away from family and friends for the holiday season. They will have a turkey dinner served in a chow line far from home and a prayer will be said to protect our troops while carrying out their mission. At home there will be an empty place at the dinner table and a prayer will be said to protect our troops and guide them to a safe return. There will be soldiers preparing to deploy and there will be soldiers returning home. There will be soldiers from other wars who will remember, with some telling their story and others just wanting to forget. Some of us will receive medals and a flag to take home and others will go home under a draped flag. There will be talk of peace on earth and good will toward men and someone will die a senseless death from a bomb or a bullet. My goal is to carry out my mission and my Christmas Wish is to be granted a day where I could sleep late and not wake-up during the night searching for my weapon, to eat a meal with real utensils and plates that clink, and food that doesn't churn in my stomach. One day where every person that I meet has all their limbs, a day where nobody gets hurt and nobody dies. Just one day for Peace on Earth and Good Will for everyone.

Dreams Undone

Now that we have been to a world of dreams
We must awake to a world of reality
Where all is evolved around a turbulence
of disorder.
Trees are few and flowers........are none.

The sun is blocked by dark black clouds
surrounded in a dismal gray.
The air, heavy with fumes and dust held
suspended in an aqueous mist that gives
you a feeling of depression....
a depression that prostrates your soul
to the ground.

The foreboding buildings erupt into
freeways patched in artificial nature
sprinkled with wreckage and waist
from human progress.
Together clashing with nature to
malign all it possesses.

The mutation of nature.

A world that is musty and moldy
rotten with stench.
a world crying and laughing
without human affection.
A world that is heartless and cruel
A world full of people without faces.
A society sickened with jealously
and greed.
Lost are we in this world without color,

lost of happiness, lost of compassion.
A world..........lost of love.
To believe that we shall never dream
would be to give up life.

To live in a dream but not to live a dream.
To live not at all is not to dream.
Is he a fool that lives in a dream?
Is he a fool that dreams not at all?

Something About Sentiment

Terminus, One Summer Night

This summer night, so peaceful and calm, the earth is stilled by the vastness of the heavens. Filled with celestial wealth, the universe extends on forever, seemingly dusted with countless sparkling diamonds. Yet the darkness is hardly pierced by the canopy of twinkling gems, revealing nothing of its nightly mysteries. The night does well without the blazing sun to scorch and stir the green flourishing blooms of sculptured lawns and pampered gardens. These scents are free to drift and linger motionless in the unmoving air, subduing even the wildest disposition. The entrancing darkness possess the power to render the mind with inner peace, a calm that can only be found nearest the soul. And without the smiling moon pretending to be a less bright sun, snickering upon the earth, plays not its game of mischievously steeling the darkness from sleeping creatures. The solace of silence is barely broken by the sounds of those nocturnal things that scurry and crawl in search of nourishment and rest. This cloudless night is host to unwilling thespians acting out a cycle of nature in a harsh reality. Their brief performance goes unapplauded and is replayed over and over again, without review, without laughter or sadness, without compassion. Then the, curtain falls with the first light of day, only in the void of night will they rise again with a new cast of players repeating the same performance.

A lighted candle burns solemnly in the void of night, casting about it an amber spherical glow. Reaching out with its votive beams, the candle could only light dimly the shallow surroundings within the boundaries of its circle. Although the extent of its beam was limited, the flame reached into the darkness to touch the spirit of an unsuspecting creature. The flames unusual touch would change the way of the creature and its unusual effect would change forever the creature's life.

A moth appeared near the edge of the flickering orb. Fluttering and bouncing in erratic patterns, the moth faded in and out of the darkness. Appearing to be lost, the moth had been blinded by the brightness of the flame. It had been distracted from its path, distracted from its normal, its natural course of life. Skirting the rim of darkness, its efforts to correct its course of destination, diminished with the lure of the fiery dance of the flame. Like a honeybee drawn to a flower, the moth changed its course toward the direction of the flickering ballerina. The flame possessed an overwhelming power to have the ability to capture the moth's attention and draw it within the reaches of its influence. The moth veered and banked, flying near the flame, then away again. The moth seemed to perceive an essence of color emanating in a beautiful array about the flame. A rainbow of mesmerizing color, the moth had been captured.

The flame bound to a wick, had a center of blue which engulfed a red glow at the base of its source, symbolizing a beating heart. The blue embraced in in a yellowish orange, casting about the flame an innocent nimbus of purity, an essence expressing a desire for love.

The moth, a less attractive creature was the dullest of its kind. Its brown dusty body absent of bright color, projected a nothingness, a quality typical of unfilled space. And except for being alive, it could not be distinguished from the deciduous growth from which it came.

The moth flew past the flame once again and the flame flickered in a blushing redness. The moth, overjoyed with the response of the flame, banked and rolled and climbed high above the candle in a clumsy display of its ability to fly. With each pass, the moth so entranced in an odd courting ritual, flew closer and closer to the baking ardent. The moth began a circling path about the flame, as it pitched and yawed, positioning its wings for greater speed and stability. Its spiraling path accelerated as the distance between itself and the flame decreased. Its body shuttered as it surpassed a velocity never before experienced. The light dust of its body trailed behind and burst in a shower of sputtering brilliance as the moth glanced through the flames combustible fringes. What force has overtaken this creature's instinct for survival? What can compel a creature to surrender itself in such entirety? The adventure was new and exciting, much more than it had ever imagined, much more than it could ever resist. The temperature must have been unbearable as the moth broke from its forever closing pattern. In a staggering panic it rolled into a vertical loop, high above the candle and circled and fluttered seemingly to cool its wings. The moth had never before been confronted with such illumination, for it was drawn totally and completely toward the bouncing incandescence. The moth maintained a safe distance between itself and the flame, yet it still did not lose interest in the captivating glow. There was a confusion about the origin of the heat. Perhaps it was a barrier to be broken, a boundary to cross in order to reach the flame. Perhaps the heat was a passing thing and is no longer present.

The moth, still entranced in its hypnotic state, seemed to want nothing more than to touch the flame. Its flight became more erratic and for the moment there was and uncertainty in its actions. Maybe now it will break for the deep shade of night, return to where it came, return to live out the evening, to live out its life in the safety of darkness, in the safety of night. In an instant, it turned toward the flame, diving directly into a tight circling path with even greater speed than before. The moth pulled its legs tightly against its body and its wings rippled and twisted and began to fold against the horrific forces of its rapid descent. As the radius of its turn became smaller, the seemingly unrelenting determination toward self-destruction appeared inevitable and like suddenness of its actions it all had ended.

There was a cynical blaze of furry engulfing the moth as it reached the center of the flame. Yet for an instant, the moth appeared to be at ease as it embraced the tiny red glow. The flame displayed no triumphant reaction but instead, flickered and dimmed, maybe in pity or regret. A wave of wax rose and streamed down the side of the candle as the moth rolled and tumbled, plunging lifeless into the melted pool of wax below.

The flame was bound to its existence by what it was and the moth so different in every way had crossed the boundary by which they were separated. The flame was a comforting relief from the darkness and like the charred remains of the moth that lie motionless in a liquid grave, the candle itself would soon expire. It could be seen by the continuous flow of wax that fell like golden teardrops upon the moth, that it would be embraced within the remains of the candle. So different in their existence, now joined in a natural bond.

Love, Life, Hope and Time

Love to lovelessness,
    found and foundless.
Life to lifelessness,
    bound and boundless.
Hope to hopelessness,
    unspoken and traceless.
Time to timelessness,
    unbroken and spaceless.

Silly Sunset

Silly Sunset
I've watched you come and go
Changing night to day
And day to night
Across the earth below

Silly Sunset
A chill is in the air
The night steals another heart
And the pumpkin is covered with frost
The darkness just doesn't care

Silly Sunset
This distorted shape outgrows
A living source to fade in gray
And play this game in human form
Stretching shadows in long repose

Silly Sunset
Your golden orb has crossed
My path with memories today
Through clouds gripped by storm
Toward distant horizons to be lost
Silly Sunset

Parting

With the coming of the morning sun
The romantic ghost of night must run
To follow the ever winding maze
Quickly fading in violet haze.

And golden beams reach from far
To melt away the distant star
The sun another night to seethe
As slow the wind begins to breath.

In perfumed air from branches sweet
Yet false and true in harsh defeat
To what reason life in taking
Not the dawn but heart in breaking.

In sepulcher clouds for heaven's sake
Such peace can only morning break
In reticent reverie bound to keep
The dreams from sleep to another sleep.

Turn to gray the billowing clouds
To the day in terminus shrouds
Created illusions in nightly climes
Rings the hour in melancholy chimes.

Turn to earth the fragrant flowers
So long and empty are the hours
Like mortal daisies dropping seeds
Shall be tomorrow's winter weeds.

Bending to earth a matin bed
A mercy bell to please the dead
Lulled asleep by whispers flow
As fallen seeds are left to grow.

And quiet tones softly surge
As slow winds sing an empty dirge
To distant timbrels, a rolling thunder
As vernal visions slip coldly under.

Surrounded in such weighted grief
With sad falling tears in disbelief
To bind the season in even number
On winters eve in peaceful slumber.

With stillness and calm settled inside
Silence to silence multiplied
Blossom to blossom wither and fall
Parting is the saddest of all.

Christmas Wish 2004

During this season of Peace, Love and Joy
I find myself haunted by the ghosts of the deserts
and the emptiness of distant lands.
There are many of us training to live without a uniform and a weapon.
Learning to fit into a society divided over the winds of war.
But the horizon glows with a new light filled
with promise and encouragement.
My wish is that we can all find happiness in each and every day.
Develop the strength and wisdom to deal with the challenges of daily
life and maintain a spirit that will never give up on hopes and dreams.
To nurture a mind filled with pleasant thoughts and
wonderful memories and be blessed with a loving
heart that holds compassion for others.
I extend to all, my most warm and sincere
wishes for this holiday season.

Footprints

Part I

While my thoughts hush the roar
of the surf upon the peaceful shore
I seek a place beside the sea
where I can let my heart run free.

The sun extending in arms to reach
the sea struck sands of a lonely beach
trying to cast its shimmering beam
its votive tapers lucidly gleam.

to bring about a shadowed path
edged beside the surging wrath
so helplessly it fails to stave
the boundless sweep of a gentle wave.

Languor trail that cannot hide
from the currents of a wrestles tide
hard and swift in apt array
the imprinted sand is washed away.

Washed Away

Part II

Reminiscent swirl of failing sand
that sweeps so easy from the land
foretells of days in which we played
lost in memories that are so frayed.

Amongst the fortress of the years
at leisure testing all our tears
alone in searching stranded ways
a fallen sand castle of other days.

Imparted Myriads drawn so deep
within its depths to forever keep
to speed such thoughts to endless flow
and sink in drifting tides a glow.

Reborn enhanced in sweetness form
as calmness isn't seethed by storm
perhaps at best the ecstatic die
to the azure place known as high.

Forever Gone

Part III

Untying the darkness from the day
laves in a rainbow on its way
through the placid beauty of canopied skies
silently closing its tired eyes.

So pendulous in a moments grace
horizons touch to last embrace
with a parting kiss, and quiet hush
a sparkling smile, a surfaced blush.

Cast to me last ray of light
twinkle softly, giving way to the night
sensitive emotions though it may seem
those limners of life are but a dream.

The weary wanderer's footpath dies
for now alone the echoing cries
rings through the night a grievous call
a sorrowful song, another star did fall.

Christmas Wish 2005

The holiday season is a time of reflection and a time to renew faith.

During this time we may remember a Christmas past in faded images of a lighted tree, a special gift, a Christmas Carol or the chime of silver bells. Perhaps, reminisce about the merry times with family and friends celebrating the miracle of peace on earth and good will toward men. These thoughts may linger in a dusty memory which may return while hanging ornaments on your tree or maybe during one of those quiet moments, while lost in reflection, with a feeling that you have been touched by the spirit of Christmas.

Each year the Spirit of Christmas shines with a greater brilliance, to reach the hearts of all who will receive the gift of understanding the true meaning of the season. This effort to renew your faith in God and humanity is not only for Christmas day but for all the year that follows. My wish is that we all can experience these blessings of the season.

May the Spirit of Christmas reach your heart and be yours always.

Clouds

Rolling hills, westward pass
grazing cattle eating grass
a cloud outlined by setting sun
a horse whose form reared wild begun
to change the sky like melting snow
so brief its beauty can it show
with furled main it raised its head
and outstretched hoofs it turned and fled

Father to Son

As you go into life's wandering maze
your way to another meadow graze
unshrouded by this watching eye
what darkened path will you try?

To reach the utmost peak above
unsheltered by the hand of love
whose journey full of joy and pain
cannot be sheltered from the rain.

As briery tangles cling to teach
life's path upon the summit reach
unraveled to more pleasant ways
in search of finding happier days.

Found ambition in nameless vale
to sit someday and tell the tale
of blindly stumbling on the road
with doubtful burden to unload.

A fair faced stranger you may meet
in making all you blessings sweet
to bring your own with hope and pride
a little hand for you to guide.

Then not listen to others glory
but telling of your own life's story
that flowers cannot bloom in shade
and strength of will must never fade.

And broken promises we may regret
so soon life's lessons we may forget
that seldom do we see the strife
until we turn and look back on life.

Once a Dream

Tired eyes closing, slowly closing
Wanting to rest, to sleep
Tarry kiss of night, so quiet
Pass stillness in the soul at dusk
To quell this day in calm and
Kindle a promise of the dawn
Tryst, once a dream of soft
And soothing serenity
Once a dream so sweet.

What

What a person may like best about you
is what you do not tell them.

Learning

To think how foolish were the things done yesterday
And yesterday's thoughts were so kind.
So how then, will today seem, when tomorrow
These thoughts are gone?

Sad Day

In such horrid as sackcloth been
As ashes put to rest.
In nearly all the world has touched
Within its grasp a flowing tear
And lambent thoughts to
Remain at peace in cerements
Dress, unfound but
Not forgotten.

Natural

Each year divided
In half and half again
One somewhat rainy
One somewhat dry
One somewhat hot
One somewhat cold
Occurring in proper time
All four being natural.
A door is opened
A door is closed
A life begins
A life ends
Occurring in proper time
All for being natural.........

I will know when my life is fulfilled.

Seasons

Colors of the winter make me want to sleep,
Footsteps frozen, slowed by winters cold.

Colors of the spring make me want to dance,
Footsteps free, everything new and blooming.

Colors of the summer make me want to walk,
Footsteps moving on, the land maturing fast.

Colors of the autumn make me want to think,
Footsteps silent, in falling leaves to reminisce.

Sorrow

Sorrow is explained as a sadness or anguish due to a loss. It is a grief or sense of guilt that implies pain caused by a deep disappointment.

Of all the unavailing remorse, nothing of past can be changed. And knowing how it would end does not relieve this fruitless longing. For these conscious events that make up life will be lost eventually to memory, which in itself is sad but sadder still is not knowing what had been lost.

Flying

Upside down the clouds would be
A snow cover plan, so far to see
The earth and sky their places changed
To fall above is nothing strange.

To rest your head upon the ground
And spread your arms to fly around
And roll upon cloud stuffed pillows
Beyond the rain and soot tinted billows.

And glide above the enormous gray
As the fading sun is sealed away
Not too close to the day or night
Just indifferent, to black or white.

Sailing the skies eternal hue
Around the world in sonic blue
Transcending, a portrait of the land
Captured only by the artist hand.

Briefly brushed in pictured lines
The velvet touch of emerald pines
Over summer's valley's warm below
Or winter's mountains covered with snow.

The blissful blooms of yellow and pink
In beaming waves from the heavens sink
To the beginning of a sightless spring
Where homeless birds sweetly sing.

Entwined; the never ending story
For what is real within this glory
Could bring such hope to earth and sky
With spreading wings, a wish to fly.

Oh this day of childish fun
In fantasy play until setting sun
To rest this soul upon a snowy peak
And quietly listen to memories speak.

Once Young

Of weary taunt, remote unfound
To lay upon the humble ground
Untouched in ease of aspirant dream
Removed, not all the malignant stream
In flow through the transient field
Inspiring such as youth could yield.
Remorse, aesthetic, never shown
To those who see, yet remain unknown.

Look

I looked into the mirror and I liked
what I saw, then everything was okay.

Nova

Upon the threshold of a star
Nothing near you all so far
So placid is your shining beam
An elusive dream upon a dream

Captured bits of sparkling light
Dancing in the peaceful night
Is it there or has it gone
Yet in hope or is there none.

Entangled in your vibrant lure
Residing on your distant shore
Profound emotions turning gray
Betwixt devotion must it stay?

Amidst the binding of its place
To find yourself in soul disgrace
Against the soul committing crime
In space forgotten pursuing time.

Relieved of all its tensile strain
Hidden by the falling rain
Of how it is or was is seen
In traces past of what has been.

No more do things of meaning stir
The memory loss of what they were
The feelings lost remain concealed
As aspired visions, are never revealed.

Heart and soul to bath in lust
To what vexation turn to dust
Bequeathed a love to wills last breath
Fall to silence and surrender to death.

No Space

There is no space between heaven and earth, just an eternity.

Christmas Wish 2006

The Christmas rush is on as we race to put up our trees and decorations, prepare for the holiday feast and shop feverishly for that last minute gift. I can't tell you how many times I found myself at the mall on Christmas Eve wondering what to buy and watching the stores close. The years have taught me to start my shopping early, but not how to remember where I stashed the stuff. The day after last Christmas I found a card that I was going to give to Gina, so I told her that I would save it for this year, but now I can't remember where I put it. I tried writing myself notes, but after going through the wash they end up in waded balls at the bottom of the pockets.

Gina's girls still have that innocent belief in Santa Claus, which is fun to watch on Christmas morning and insures me of some cookies and milk on Christmas Eve. It is something that I really look forward to even though I am lactose intolerant.

Dane Jr is over six feet tall and now drives. With any luck maybe he will let me borrow his car. Although I no longer spend time putting his gifts together on Christmas Eve, I still look forward to watching him open his gifts and he is even more willing to let me have a turn playing with some of the neat stuff.

I enjoy this time of the year more than any other holiday because people seem to change.

If only for a short time most people seem much nicer. I might say that wrapping gifts is a pain in the bottom, but the truth is I really enjoy wrapping gifts and anticipating the smiles they bring on Christmas morning. Of course, I get to open a few things myself and perhaps I may get some special treats in my stocking. A box of prunes would help a bit, Avodart and maybe some little blue pills to perk up the season, if you get my drift.

The Christmas reruns on television are always enjoyable, even though I have seen them hundreds of times. I especially get a chuckle out of Scrooge (Alastair Sim) standing on his head and the old lady running away with her apron over her face. The animated stories of "The

Night Before Christmas" and the Grinch are fun to watch. Tim Allen's, "The Santa Claus" is also funny.

You know it might sound silly, but every Christmas Eve, before bed, I find myself peeking out the window with hopes of seeing a sled being pulled by nine reindeer (we can't forget the one with red nose) driven by a jolly little fat guy in a red suit and hearing a cheerful Ho, Ho, Ho.

Well, you never know.

I wish that your Christmas will be as joyous as mine.

Merry Christmas,

Stone White

Of the diseased mind from the book of Thoth
we are strewn to the corners of forbidden fear
alone in our hearts, alone in our minds
endlessly pursuing and being pursued.

Through the corridors of coriander
betwixt the emotional strain of
submissive destitute unto the arms
of passive invocation, never to freed
from the desolate the chambers.

The gimmick now drawn of repulsive
sensations, where to look on as high
is benign and malignant, with a taste
of a simple pure sympathy.

In retreat of the deed, from the sack
of molded illusions, now live
in a world of canopy skies, until
the moment you find, with life
you no longer have ties.

"la morte saida tutti I conti"
(death pays all debts)

To Look On As High

The flickering candle light bouncing shadows across the walls and ceiling, appearing as ghostly images, dancing in a shadowy apparition. A dramatic spectacle mysteriously performing a ceremonious ritual. The fragrance of incense fills the air suggesting the attempt to conceal the odor of burning dried leaves. The muffled sounds of distant music filter through a veil of hallucinating smoke. A cloud which encircles your mind like a floating disembodied spirit to converge with your senses and create an air of pensive quietude. A wedge of orange sunshine drives furiously into your brain, separates infinitely, splitting into factions your every thought and dislodging your imagination, transporting it in every conceivable direction. Deranged, in a state of confusion, reality and fantasy have overlapped.

Illusions... Dreams... Night...Day...Live...Die.

Hard so soft, sweet so warm bitter as cold, free, and free as the wind...chained to the earth. Trees of stone that do not grow, a lost bumble bee with wheels. Singing birds fly without wings. A lonely pumpkin by the sea. Reach down to touch they sky. A tombstone crushed by a feather. To despoil of purity a fallen tear drop shatters. Extending far downward, backward from life.

Sense the warmth of the sun, deceived for the sun is not there reconvened in the shadow of death, the end of existence seems near. Before a pit of fire, a caller from shades below. A flaming sword has slashed the soul, the immortal gold must flow.

"SPEAK NOT OF LIFE!" "FOR YOU HAVE LIVED YOUR EXSISTANCE IN ITS ENTIRETY, EXPOSING THAT WHICH HAVE BURIED DEEP IN THE DARKEST CAVERNS OF YOUR MIND".

You have taken for granted even that which seems ever so common. Taken by devious means that which you desired most and could not possess. You have not loved ever completely to which you were ordained. You have been vindictive for the miseries of your hatred. Hatred which has consumed your person. Hatred, which has withdrawn you into yourself, receded near death, so that the diabolical within you has risen to stand victorious upon your grave.

No situation will seem as intolerable as that which you now confront. For your reserves are exhausted and the end of human existence is upon you. Now you must face condemnation.

With overpowering apprehension, your thoughts are transversed in swoon to a dark void. Cast to the extent of space, time, and the unknown. You are only to fear yourself, for you are your own enemy. This scared soul has an eternity of silence in which to ponder and burn in emptiness from its own iniquities. The evilness of life, shall echo within your soul into infinity.

Life is only temporary and body made of clay. Birth did give the living soul a body for a home. For it is from dust we came and dust we shall return.

The sounds which were once music, have been played out to a deafening silence. The combating odors of dried leaves and incense, have been reduced to ashes. Layers of smoke in the form of a spirit worn repose, ride unmovingly in stilled air. A tiny glow from a smoldering candle faintly drawing its last breath. It has long since exhausted its food for existence. All have served their purpose in man's material world. All have exhausted their reserves.

"Raison D'Etre Est Passe"

Christmas Wish 2007

The holiday season is upon us once again. It certainly seems the years are passing by more quickly these days. Where does the time go? I'm sure you would like to have a penny or should I say dollar, for every time you have heard that line.

With Christmas displays sprouting shortly after Halloween, we are cleverly being nudged into Christmas spending as Yule tide carol's and decked halls to loosen our purse strings. It hardly seems that Thanksgiving receives adequate time before it is ushered aside by sleigh bells ringing and chestnuts roasting on an open fire. Children may be snug in their beds but the parents are dreading the after Christmas blues, as visions of dollar signs dance in their heads. "Ah gees!" I can see Archie Bunker now, with a cringed facial expression uttering, "Christmas is at our throats again!" Well, not everyone is immediately touched by the Christmas spirit. Even Scrooge held out until Christmas Eve before having a change of heart. With good reason, we never seem to hear very much about those uninspired grouches who never become enlightened by the Christmas spirit.

I suppose we would like to believe that everyone has a soft side. Yet, there are still some unbelieving souls that will go to their graves blabbering bah-humbug. You can rest assure these hard-hearted Hannibal's will never rate a television special or fairytale. Certainly good reason why they never made Grimm's list! So if you are feeling a little grumpy and are dreading the holiday season, you may not want to wait until Christmas Eve to change your mood. Surely if you wait until the last minute, you may find yourself listening to the cries of those lost souls shadowed in the clanging turmoil of Jacob Marley's chains, blaming your nightmare on a morsel of undigested beef. After which you may be destined to spend a night with the three Christmas spirits. Rumor has it; these three are tougher in person, especially the quiet one decked in black, with the boney fingers.

As for me, I don't need a brick to drop on my head! The outside lights have been put up and although it has seen better days, the Christmas tree is all decorated. Maybe I'll catch an after Christmas sale on an artificial spruce. I also have a good start on my Christmas shopping, with only a few minor purchases left to search out. It should be wrapping paper and labels from here on in. No telling what I have forgotten, but I'm sure I'll remember sooner or later. Come to think of it, I never did find that Christmas card I misplaced last year. Nevertheless, I'll be having fish on Christmas Eve and before bed a routine glance of the sky before closing the shutters should prove to be a silent night.

MERRY CHRISTMAS

Reflection, I

The air is cold and still
To a darkness across the hill
With an emptiness to fulfill
The illusions of another day.

Beginning indeed beneath the tower
To sit alone at vesper hour
In hand a dried and wilted flower
Turning back in time another day.

The castle's bell has lost its tone
Walls of ivy and sculptured stone
Mystic tears through starlight shone
Falling from granite eyes.

Whispering wind into my ear
Words that one should want to hear
From actors apparitions lingering near
The amphitheaters stage.

Such ghostly shadows to enfold
Fading memories to behold
For just an instant to unfold
Your dreams in rounded sleep.

Relief is welcomed as the rhyming sound
Of roaring chariots echoing abound
Disappear into silence so profound
The past begins to sweep.

Through a pane of glass, to an autumn past
A day in September
Upon a rock beside a stream
So pleasant to remember
Hours of forgotten cares
Sunlight in the sand
Is only such that youth could share
Though never understand.

The revels now begin
As actors to foretell
Its substance taken
From air so thin
Its basic fabric remains unseen

"They played and played throughout the day
Wondering if a kiss would change the way
Life's sweet intent creeps in its sullen pace
Is somehow soothed within a warm embrace."

Before the ambers grasp
Submitted to the autumns clasp
The crossing of two destinies
Were bronzed upon the golden leaves.

Love held the time that followed
As the prolific past was swallowed
In passions-play pretending, intending
A love to last, but never ending?

Could such a love endure till then?
As passion slips to know not when
Like calmer seas beneath the ocean
Is often see in gentle motion.

To see your gaze laced in sorrow
Will you still love me tomorrow?
The unfathomed depth of feeling
Waiting, wasting never revealing
Reflections in the rivers flow....
Speak softly, never let go
The mountains peak is covered with snow
And the cries of the dying
Tender hearts forever crying
While the night wind sweep away another soul.

-And never linked to error trust
That someday end, as it must
With lovers hearts consumed in dust
Left hanging in fire and wind.

As loneliness to the sunset slips
From my arms, from my lips
On wilder seas and sinking ships
Of all that thunders in a wave.

Tomorrow, tomorrow, forever tomorrow
There will always be, but not: for the
Word is none or not to be....
What questions do trouble the mind?

A gull upon the frozen shore
The ice glazed sands to be once more
To change a day and wonder how
Where is nature's kindness now?

Ever changing rapid pace
Something in the mirrors space
Treasures lost within such sleep
Heaven trembles when angels weep.

Lady of the morning mist
Wither flowers from your kiss
Whose pedals after June must die
Have you wondered if I cry?

Of all that's gone and couldn't save
The cherished from a genial grave
Shall peace illume in kindness light
All that's hidden in darkest night.

While the clouds receded to a soft dying day
An angel's tear was kissed from her check
Then to sleep like children in a fairytale.

-Into a pond two stones were tossed
Splashing to rounding ripples, crossed
The subsiding circles quietly lost
Becoming mixed elements of the past.

The airs of different directions
Calm the restless uneven emotions
Constantly changing complexions
Blended in marbled skies.

Withering to voiceless shadows
In the darkness while they weep
Residing with the dead and half living
Left summers mood in castle keep.

As shattered silence pierced the air
In hope the real seem more clear
Through silver dust and reappear
As gold beams and still images.

In continuous reels of dried melodies
Reflecting some uncertainties
"On the dark side of the moon"
And feel that always the end is soon.

The castle would still stand
Were it not for a grain of sand
Lost to the wind.

Reflection, II

Dark night and shadows fall
Repeating voices in the hall
Answer creatures to the call
In the sounds of sorrow

Cold winds bring a winter's chill
Echo's softly from the hill
To a love that lingers still
Though lighted, candelabra's dim.

The curtain raised upon the stage
The music roared in a fit of rage
Fretting their time inside a cage
Those holy banners waved.

Lonely as they climbed the stairs
Two hearts loosely tied in pairs
Sadly hung on empty chairs
As their tears are dried.

Within this dream does stillness lift
Through closing eyes a vision sift
In tide-less sleep a stillness drift
Soft and silent peace.

Those players are now dancing
In the shadows quietly prancing
Secretly seemly chancing
Ever to be seen.

The browning grass could never last
In the cold of December
Or could a key unlock an elusive dream
A dream or burning ember
To seek the warmer airs
Still within this land
Should smolder love so unaware
Slow in burning firebrand.

And to the revels of this vision
Melting to the air
So riddled poor fool with questions
Alone in silent prayer.

Every minute, every hour
Every moment so dear
Ever passing, never lasting
The morning grows near.

-When all the world is asleep
They venture like children
Beyond the fence, seeking
The realms of haunting fear
Or the kingdoms of perfect joy-

In what mystery to the blind
With eyes that see but cannot find
A heart alone or faith within
To save them from a sea of sin.

Sermons sung from distant temples
And from the tempest faded
Pallid under crying skies
The castle is now shaded
Inherited by those solemn spirits
Seen shivering in the wind
A topple tower and palace
Not knowing they have sinned.

Through the distance of the years
Blowing winds will dry our tears
As time removes some childish fears
Mending a withered heart.

Like marbles on a table tilting
Melting snow or flowers wilting
Capriciously to feel the jilting
As these seconds pass.

The midnight hour to bestill
Growing colder from the chill
Hollow meaning, weakened will
An angel's call to sleep

To be a prisoner of this dream
Facing the flames of hell
To the shock of dark emptiness
Lost within a timeless spell.

Ticking, ticking of the clock
Seconds passing through the lock
Never pausing, never causing
Time to stop, no time to stop
The hands and fingers of the clock

To pursue its long endeavor
Clashing, clanging on forever
Equal and even must it sever
Each passing moment of time.

Tossed and turned in restless sorrow
As its hands reach for tomorrow
Not a second lend or borrow
Each passing moment of time.

In the glory of its ticking
Marching rhythm always ticking
Never slowing never picking
Up a second for its rhythm.

Cruelly taking what we treasure
To burn and freeze all our pleasure
In gauging order can it measure
On the hour in its chime.

Passing numbers in its pace
Never turning to retrace
With no emotion on its face
The past at last becomes sublime.

To the ticking, ticking clicking of the clock
Keeping time, taking time, time to stop
No time to stop the endless ticking of the clock.

Audible ticking, lightly tapping
Austere, ascetic, repeatedly rapping
Fades in muffled madness trapping
All that ever was before
All that was and is no more
In the closing of the door
To be balanced against infinity.

Forgetting is meaningless

A Better Way

What is it that I can tell you, to help you find a better way?
Maybe some meaningful words of wisdom
to keep you from going astray
Or something kind to recognize the goodness in your heart
As forgiving thoughts can take away a taste that is very tart

How can I explain why happiness is tempered so by sorrow
Or tell you that, although it hurts, the pain will fade tomorrow
There is an answer why bumble bees fly
and the morning songs of birds
But to tell you why life can be so cruel, I just haven't got the words

I cannot take you to the rainbows end or lead you to a better place
So you must care about yourself before another you can embrace
Yet, at this moment I must confess that life will take its toll
You must believe what counts the most is the love within your soul.

Christmas Wish 2008

To wish someone a Merry Christmas usually comes across as, Have a Happy Holiday, Good Cheer, Make Merry or just crack open another bottle of Jack! We all have become accustomed to buying gifts, putting up a tree and decorations or" here's to it and to it again, etc." whatever! At the risk of offending a few, I would like to express, what I believe, is the true meaning of Christmas.

A long time ago, this Angel came to announce to the earth that "I bring good news and joy which will be for all the people". This angel was telling of a Savior who is the Christ the Lord, and on that day will be born in the city of David; he will be born a King that will transform the world. So we have Christmas, The "mas", being the mass of Christ.

It was on this day that the spiritual atmosphere of the earth was transformed. Yet, today some are offended if you wish them a Merry Christmas, so what do we do? Do we give in and play it safe by just saying Happy Holiday or do we take that risk and say "I wish you a Merry Christmas? Has it come to the point that we should wear a tag proclaiming that is or isn't okay to wish me a Merry Christmas?

The good news is that "Good Always Triumphs Over Evil" and the light of this new world will overshadow the rulers of the darkness.

This past year I have experienced enormous personal and material losses, yet gained an even greater spirituality, that will light my path to a higher awareness.

There will be no Christmas cookies and milk for me this year but I will thank God for the birth of Christ and before bed check the skies for the little fat guy in the red suit with his sleigh and reindeer.

My Christmas wish for you is, May the light of your higher power, your God, your Savior, redeem you from the forces of darkness and light your path to the right side of the Broad Road and be not ashamed to wish anyone or everyone a Merry Christmas.

Forgotten

Surely it is a kindness
that we may be blessed
with mortality, knowing
our tired bones may rest
dumb to the meaningless
words of snickering shadows.
Then could life be so cruel
to end a quest, a feeble quest
that exist within the struggling
madness of jagged minds.
Tormented by a forgotten pilgrimage
in pursuit of a perfect happiness,
a tragic love ends in disappointment,
only to be resorbed in emptiness.

Journeys End

Alone this verse will end
unpoetic in its charm,
empty in decaying muse.
The tittering thief of time
smiles while being paid
as another line is etched
upon your face and another
precious moment is stolen.
A callus conclusion unfolds to
those tenured in earthly space
by a limited segment of life.
So slowly the empty spirit
moves with shuffling steps
nearer the journeys' end.

Time To Rest

Maddening is the thought
that cannot grasp the illusive
image changed by paler
shadows by the rising stars.
what thought is pictured of
this earth at a distance half
way round its circle.
This soft sweet angel stands weary
upon the shore, peering into the east.
Then tired eyes turn toward the
setting sun, whose beams glaze
red upon rosy cheeks. Far away
hell-hounds pursue another prey,
It is our time to rest.

Christmas Wish 2010

Here we go again!

I still need to do some Christmas shopping and most of the sporting good stores are out of ammo, so an alternate list would certainly be helpful. I haven't sent out Christmas cards or bought a tree but if need be I have my Charlie Brown back-up. The refrigerator has no beer but there is some dead stuff in the freezer that will make a fine Christmas dinner.

I have a new format in Microsoft word and I have yet to find spell check. And this is all recent stuff. The past year has been filled with many challenges yet they didn't seem burdensome.

MERRY CHRISTMAS

To my sweet Angel;

In the beginning, we agreed to a promise to be as one, which nothing could or would come between us. But you declined to turn away other interest. I thought we could be enough for each other, that we would focus on the future and maybe you would decide that I was enough for you. But I presumed wrong, I could just never mean all that much to you. You were not "My Angel" and you would never be mine. We promised never to go to sleep without a kiss good night and promised to talk about what was bothering us before we laid to rest. But when I told you what bothered me and what hurt my feelings. Like a hopeless puppy, I expected a kind word and reassurance that everything was okay; instead you continually got angry and chastised me for being jealous or insecure. It became easier to just hurt and turn away. Eventually, turning away became routine and the hurt, I wrongly thought, more bearable. Just like it was easier for you to react viciously rather than with kindness and reassurance. The cause and effect was upside down.

So "false and true in harsh defeat", resulted in just the opposite of my wish and my breaking another promise. Maybe it was then that you lost your respect for me.

I suppose your message was clear but maybe because of an addictive relationship or some other reason that I may have for denying the truth, I can only now see the empty future. The result is facing an end to something that never really began and losing something I never really had.

What I believed to be a dream come true, a second chance at true love has come to nothing. All that I thought was real is nothing more than an illusion, an erroneous perception of reality that can exist only in the hearts and minds of profound dreamers and fools. Of all the misconceptions in life, this by far is the cruelest experience the heart could endure. It is just another tale of an idiot shuffling in his daily pace, living from day to day in phantom shadows, only to find a hollow death, in autumn tone as futile as a dry leafs falling to the ground.

"Illusions, dreams, night, day, live, die, hard so soft, sweet so warm, bitter so cold". The Moth is entombed in wax and the bumblebee has no wings but floats on a snowflake high above a mountain peak to swirl in spiraling winds forever above an empty place.

The snowflake carrying my dream has melted away and the wish made beneath the bright star in heaven has faded with the beat of a drum and a sounding trumpet.

Bound to Woodridge, these sparkling crystals crack, while trying to reach the threshold of the distant star, they have drifted in barren space only to again become a lighted memory, only to again fall to rest on the Dark Side of the Moon.

Then again, should I have expected anything different?

This tragedy of two hearts cheated of an eternal love lies in the meaningless words of endless affection and the forlorn dream of living happily ever after. Hearts like ours will eventually grow old and die, crumbling to dust like the tattered pages of rhyme and verse that told of a fruitless bond, never to know the forever love, never to remember we once have loved, never to remember we once have loved each other.

This grand illusion has been created by the strongest of wills and the deepest desires of two souls pursuing the greatest passion and long after these living bodies are gone, the essence of what might have been will be seen in the stars and felt in the wind and these faithful spirits will eventually inherit the earth at a time when the world is meant to embrace such beauty, and be free to live and love again, to embrace as one, so that together we may relive the most beautiful of sunsets.

So life is bound to a passing memory. The memory of you and all I thought we were together. You once said that you love me; you love me so much that it hurts. You said that you will always love me and that the sun will never set even one day, without you thinking of me, or were you thinking of some other passing vision. You said that I would always have a piece of your heart. But it isn't just a piece of your heart that I want, it isn't just a piece of your heart that I need.

This spirit, slow to learn, sleeps in the gathering of seven angels, cold and still under a blanket of fresh fallen snow, mumbling a prayer for forgiveness, praying for faith, praying for eternal life.

So empty and alone are these times we are apart, that a day seems like an eternity, so endless and dreary, with only the night to ease the burden of lighted hours. This waking time slows to near stillness as the lines upon my face deepen with every passing second, yet seemingly speeds so frantically to a dusty end. Only the thought of closing eyes and rest, to dream, to dream again as before, can save the fragile foundation of a lifelong passion from the currents of lost hope and the chill of a lost memory. This sanctuary exists only behind closed eyes, in the realm of sleep, to dream in the protection of sleep, the pleasure of sleep, free from the madness and turmoil of this frantic world, free to dream peacefully, forever in peace.

Existing only until dawn, the tales stemming from my dreams will lead to a happier end, holding your hand, breathing the sweet night air. Somewhere on the edge of night, the rising sun chases blurred shadows through opaque windows of a castle dark and there my spirit lingers and there my spirit weeps.

"As loneliness from the sunset slips from my arms, from my lips"… "tomorrow, tomorrow, forever tomorrow there will always be but not, for the word is none, or not to be".

And so it is "To Late The Rain"

God's Love for us has allowed our hearts to touch, but we were lost in ourselves and I didn't know that it is only by his Grace and a strong belief in the Holy Spirit that we can truly love, truly Love each other and allow ourselves to be loved.

This morning, before opening my eyes, I rolled over to put my arm around you and you weren't there. Only then did I realize that you would never be.

I Love You As Always
Good-Bye

Christmas Wish 2010

The ancient story begins in Bethlehem over 2000 years ago. We celebrate the birth of One who brings salvation for mankind.

Three wise men brought gifts to a child, and the child would in turn give all a chance for eternal life.

The child would be the incarnation of the perfect Being and become a teacher, prophet and a leader of all mankind.

He would teach love and forgiveness. He would inspire Faith, Hope, Charity and the fruit of being righteous.

In the centuries that have past, this celebration has evolved and grown, to include a little fat guy in a red suit, who flies around the world in one night giving gifts to children.

Unbelievable as it sounds, the job still gets done. The season begins to fill with joy as lighted decorations and all sorts of ornaments cover houses, yards and Christmas trees. People frantically buy gifts and children write endless lists of toys and things they would like Santa to leave under their Christmas trees. We give, we receive; enjoy feasting and fellowship and holiday cheer. Whether we are alone on Christmas morning or with family and friends, all those who believe will, in some way be moved by the Holy Spirit, the Christmas Spirit.

Isn't it amazing, that after 2000 years, we still bring gifts and celebrate the birth of the new born King? Certainly, this must be more than a ritual, tradition or a chance to break from monotonous routines. It must be the testimony of Truth! John 18:37 Jesus said; "I was born into this world to testify the truth". How else could such a concept survive from a single instance if it were not true?

This year I wish for all to experience the comfort, joy and inner peace provided by the Holy Spirit.

Merry Christmas

To Late The Rain

On empty days what can be seen
Through vacant eyes falls in between
The jumbled words of a poets rhyme
And remnants of a wish lost in time

In rumbling skies dark clouds advance
As course drops of furry wildly dance
Across the dry earth in blowing wind
Lightning grips a heart to exscind

A solemn spirit upon a distant peak
Flowing pendants gem on a cheek
As clouds fill with pathetic tears
And lonely hours seem like years

A careless sun whose scorching beams
Burn longing hearts with faded dreams
And barren earth whose seeds have dried
In dusty fields, the flowers have died.

Blind

The color of a rose means nothing to
a blind man, but he is open to its scent.

Christmas Wish 2011

"And there were shepherds living out in the fields nearby, keeping watch over their flocks at night. An angel of the Lord appeared to them, and the glory of the Lord shone around them, and they were terrified. But the angel said to them, "Do not be afraid. I bring you good news that will cause great joy for all the people. Today in the town of David a Savior has been born to you; he is the Messiah, the Lord." (Luke 2:8-11)

Should something like this happen today, you would surely think that you were about to be abducted by aliens! So how do you react to fear? Surely these guys had the dog dirt scared out of them, but the Angel said; "Do not be afraid'. Well, they must have had faith, because there was nothing mentioned about them being scared to death. So faith must be the key.

Daily, we are thrust into time wasting fears, as we scurry from one place to another, rushing to work, making monthly payments, bad news on the radio, fixing the car, a leaky roof, bad news from the doctor, all in an endless sea of challenges and worries that invade even our sleep. But God says, "FEAR NOT"! Okay, I say to myself. He has got to be kidding! Yet, all this worry and fear will not add one second to your lifespan. So what do we do? The good book consistently says, "Not to worry". Jesus said: "Why be like the pagans who are so deeply concerned about these things? Your heavenly Father already knows all your needs, and He will give you all you need from day to day if you live for Him and make the Kingdom of God your primary concern" (Matt. 6:33-34). Should we face each day with this in mind and a great faith in our hearts, we will be blessed with the inner peace that we need to ease the burdens in and throughout our lives. The bottom line is that we must use our faith to overcome our fears.

My Christmas wish for this holiday season is for all to hesitate, if just for a moment, to realize that we have a savior, the messiah. And all we need do is accept him with faith so that he will remove the fears, protect and guide us throughout our lives.

Merry Christmas

The Sunset and the Sea

The sun falls silent in a solemn sky
The ocean laps waves on swirling sand
Wash away drip castles, made by hand
Makes smooth the grains upon the land
Seabirds glide above a quiet blue
And gulls stand still in quiet hue
The sun falls silent, smiling but shy
As the night begins to peel away the day
Clearing the heavens of blue and gray
Draping the sea in dark array
Embraced in such a secluded haven
Shine twinkling stars in the darkest heaven
Unlocking a poetic rhyme for Raven.
The sun falls silent to bid the day goodbye.

"Is it a fool who falls in love so deeply that your entire being is consumed in a reckless desire to pursue something which has flown away? Bordering on obsession the maddening feelings can drive you to insanity, doing things beyond normality. Then one day another steps into your life and you believe that you could love again but will you cast those memories aside, will you learn to live again, will you learn to love again?"